BUDGETING
THE RIGHT WAY

The Essential Guide to Saving Money and
Living the Frugal Life

Daniel Wells

DEDICATION

This book is dedicated to those in search of an effective way to budget their money by mastering proper money management.

CONTENTS

INTRODUCTION

Some of the most frequently asked personal finance questions during this difficult economy revolve around "how to budget", "how to make a budget" and "how to live on a tight budget". Budgeting your money successfully is crucial to flourishing in any type of economy, much less a tough one. There is a common misconception that good budgeting depends upon fancy forms, financial expertise, software programs and solely on one's income. All of these false notions completely circumvent the only true goal of any personal budget: Getting the most value for each of your hard-earned dollars.

Those misguided beliefs above are the key reasons why many people are much worse off than they should be, regardless of income levels or familiarity with financial software. There are many people who are much "better off" with a lower income and a simple budget form than those with great salaries and top-notch computer programs. These successful folks are the ones who have learned the secret

CHAPTER 1 – WHY BUDGETING IS SO IMPORTANT

Budget is defined as an estimate of income and expenditure for a particular period. It is created to accomplish personal, family, organization, business and government objectives successfully within threshold of allocated fund. With proper budgeting, every cent is utilized. It charters allotted money to pay, build or complete list of targets.

It is a financial plan with list of regular expenses and designated amount for each of them. It is a personal management plan which aims to achieve financial goals without sacrificing present necessities. It is usually applied to manage household bills and essential expenses such as food, education, mortgage, transportation. A realistic budget motivates a person to designate certain amount of money for his goals.

Budget is also defined as limited supply of something. Money-wise, it means utilizing certain amount for vital need. Budget helps you focus on priorities and decide when to act on secondary needs. It is a concrete guide on how to use your money before spending it. By building a budget, you are building your future financial freedom.

Budgeting is your key to financial independence. When you budget your money, you learn smart spending. You make the most of your money by spending on what are important and necessary. You learn to delay gratifications and wait for perfect time to have them.

Here are 10 reasons why budgeting is important:

1.   It helps you reach financial goals. Budgeting makes you see the over-all picture of your monthly finances. It shows how your money comes in and goes out of your wallet. You will realize that there are certain items that take most of your money. You will also see how you are living your life. Your lifestyle influences your spending habits. Spending a lot for your wants will keep you away from your future goals. Effective budgeting can help you make them come true.

2.   It stops overspending. Without budget, you do not realize that you are spending more than what you actually have. You even spend without paying actual money. Credit cards are tools that lure you to overspend. Reality hits hard when you find out that most of your paycheck are used to pay credit cards purchases. And due to shortage of cash, you use your credit cards again to pay for gas, groceries and other needs. It leads to unhealthy spending habits and overspending. The cycle goes on and on. The best thing to do is stop using credit cards and stick to your budget.

3.   It helps you save money. Budgeting is an excellent way to save money regularly. Consider saving as part of your monthly expenses. Pay them every month like your bills. Forget about it so you will not be tempted to withdraw the fund unless for emergency purposes. When you used it, consider it as a loan and pay it as soon as money comes. Savings bring peace of mind. Keep on saving for every financial goal you want to attain.

4.   It helps you build wealth. Investing now for your future is important. When you have clear picture on what you want to have in your future life, you will start re-directing your efforts to build personal wealth. It means eliminating debts and unnecessary purchases that can affect your efforts to pursue your goals. Learn how to invest your money. When you invest, you earn passive income from interest rates or dividends. When you re-invest your earned money, you continue building your financial success. You are also motivated to increase the amount of money you invest to reach your targets quickly.

5.   It helps you plan your retirement with confidence. Budgeting now will help you build a solid retirement plan. Making plans on what you envision your life after retirement is vital. The future is unknown but it helps when you have something to lean on. Retirement fund ensures comfortable life when you become old. Investing $100 a month now for retirement fund, IRA or 401(k) will bring you benefits to enjoy life after long years of employment. It is better to be safe than sorry.

6.   It prepares you for possible emergencies. Save for your emergency fund. It helps during unexpected loss of job, sickness, injuries and other family problems that lead to financial difficulties. The ideal emergency fund is 3 month or 6 months of your monthly expenses. With this fund, you will be able to attend to your problems without

borrowing money from other people. It will help your daily needs while looking for another job or recuperating from illness and injuries. Building your emergency fund is important but you can start small by saving $10-20 a week.

7.   It helps you change your spending habits. When you make a budget, you are forced to review how you spend your hard-earned cash. You will notice that buying daily cup of latte from your favorite coffee shop is straining your monthly budget for more essential things. You do not need to stop drinking it if it is your comfort drink or awake your senses in the morning but you can create alternative like preparing your own home-made coffee version. This way, you can reduce the amount you spend for them and save money. Budgeting allows you to be smart and critical of your own spending habits. It helps you re-focus your efforts towards your financial goals by practicing better spending habits.

8.   It keeps you from worrying. Budgeting allows you to monitor your financial capacity to pay bills, purchase necessities and finance daily expenses. With budget, you can control your finances and manage all your needs. When you are in control, you can focus on your work better and sleep better.

9.   It brings peace of mind. Budgeting puts everything in order. When you list down your expenditures and allocate money to finance them, you know that everything you purchase is essential. When you allocate fund to finance something like a brand new TV or new car, you know your over-all budget will not be affected because you plan it well. It makes you enjoy your new projects or new purchases without being guilty of redirecting funds from other items on the checklist to get them.

It motivates you to focus on your long-term goals. It builds up your self-discipline by not buying the latest gadget in the market and continue saving for a new car. By keeping your eyes on the prize, you become wiser when it comes to spending your money.

Daniel Wells

CHAPTER 2 - SETTING UP A BUDGET -THE RIGHT WAY

Budgeting is simple. You can use paper and pen to create your personal or family budget. You can use online finance software to track your expenditures which help you customize your own budget plan. Popular software are Microsoft Money, Budget Pulse, Quicken, AceMoney and Mint.

An effective budget is not about complex maze of categories, numbers and dates. Basically it includes your regular expenses, spending money for daily expenses, savings and the amount you allocate for them. When you estimate funds to cover each item, it is better to put high amount. You can adjust it next month after getting hold of all incurred expenses for a month.

How to create your budget the right way? Here are 3 things to remember:

• Keep your budget simple – Identify your basic expenditures and create categories for them.

• Make it realistic – A good budget will make you manage your finances better without sacrificing essential needs. You have the control over your money and you know how to spend it wisely.

• Make it work for you - Budget helps you prepare for future expenses and save funds to finance them. Budgeting can be fun when you see how your goals manifest by learning how to save and spend smartly.

The right budget will change your spending habits and eventually alter your lifestyle. When you shift your focus from reckless spending to smart spending, you are on your way to better lifestyle in the future. Budgeting helps you make better choices to avoid previous financial problems that you encounter. It helps you see your future goals coming to realization.

Steps in Setting up Your Budget:

1. Set financial goals. Budgeting is a tool to make your goals come true. Do you want to buy a new house for your family? Do you want a new car? Do you want to take your family to a grand vacation? These goals will motivate you to start planning and manage your money.

Your goals must be realistic. You can use categories to define your goals:
- Long-term goals – 5 years or more
- Mid-term goals – 1-3 years
- Short-term goals – less than a year

Your goals must be SMART (Specific, Measurable, Achievable, Relevant and Time-framed).
- Specific- You plan to go to Italy for a vacation.

- Measurable – You need to save $ 10,000 for your trip.
- Achievable – You need to save $ 277.77 or $ 278 per month.
- Relevant – You want to reward yourself for working hard.
- Time-framed – You plan to reach this goal in 3 years.

2.   List your sources of income (salary, parents, additional jobs, allotments) and the amount you receive from them.

3.   List your expenses. To be successful in managing your own money, you need to know where it goes. Use spreadsheet and put your expenses under your categories of expenditures. Your goal is to find out how you spend your money every day. You may use general categories like:

•   Fixed Expenses – They are essential needs that need to be paid or purchased every month. It includes rent, mortgage, loans and utility bills.

•   Variable Expenses – They are necessities but adjustable needs like foods or groceries and gas expenditures.

•   Wants – These are things or activities that become habitual but not necessity.

•   Savings – It is essential for your future goals.

•   Emergency Fund – It is important to avoid financial breakdown when crisis happens in you or your family.

•   Retirement Plan /Life Insurance– Important investments to ensure comfortable life after retirement.

•   Discretionary Expenses – Optional plans such as vacation, entertainment, new gadgets like mobile phones and other little luxuries that can be eliminated or changed for practical reasons.

4.   Make a preliminary budget to start planning your financial freedom. It will help you focus on necessities rather than non-essential things.

5.   Get the sum or total of your expenses. Compare your income and expenditures. Is your expenses more than your income? Do you have monthly surplus which you can save? Do you need to work overtime to cover all your monthly expenses or ask financial assistance from your parents to pay your debts? Budgeting helps you pinpoint these things. This is also your initial step towards financial independence.

• Keep recording your expenses diligently to keep everything in order. When you need to buy something, check your budget first to know if you can afford additional expenses or delay it for a certain period.

• Adjust your budget when necessary. You have power over your budget. Reduce your wants or eliminate them to finance important things. This is important if you want to pay outstanding debts or loans. Cut down on smaller expenses to stay within your monthly budget. You can decrease frequency of your massage sessions or weekly dinner in restaurants. Save money by cooking at home or preparing home-made lunch. Check fixed expenses like cell phone plans or television package. You can reduce your monthly plans for them especially if you are not always at home to watch your favorite shows. Switch phone plans to save money. Conserve energy and use energy-saving devices to reduce your electricity bill.

Ways to Simplify Your Budget:

There are lots of ways to create a budget. One of them is applying 60-10-10-10-10% structures.

• 60% - of your income goes to your monthly expenses such as housing, utilities, food, transportation and insurance

• 10% - for your retirement plan or 401(k) investment. It is usually deducted from your paycheck when employed

• 10% - for your long-term savings. You can invest your money on index fund or stocks to gain dividends.
If you have debts to pay, you can channel this portion to pay them (home mortgage is not included because it is part of your regular expenses). Once you pay your debts, you can switch them back for your long-term goals.

This also serves as emergency fund in case of immediate family crisis.

• 10% - for your short-term savings. It is used to finance goals such as home repainting, car maintenance, medical check-up, buying gifts for special occasions and other periodic expenses. By having these savings, you will have reserved money when you need it.

10% - for your recreational or fun activities. This is important if you want to balance your life. This fund can be used to buy books, eat in a restaurant, family outing, movies or anything that you want to do. With this portion, you will not draw money from other essential categories. It is also up to you to use this fund or channel it to your long-term savings.

Daniel Wells

CHAPTER 3 - EFFECTIVE BUDGETING 101

The first rule to keep your budget effective is to stick to it. Be mindful on how you spend your money to avoid overspending. Monitor your daily expenses. Learn ways to control yourself from spending more than your budget.

Here are some ways to make your budget effective:

• Spend within your budget. If you allocated $600 for groceries in one month, then use it to shop essentials. It is better if you have a list of what you need to buy before going to grocery store to avoid buying more than you need. You can spend half of this budget and use the other half when your stocks are depleted. Just stick to the budget and do not overspend.

• Use cash for small purchases such as groceries, gas or fun expenses. Withdraw cash for your weekly expenses. When you use cash, you are not tempted to overspend. Avoid using credit cards to purchase foods or coffees. Use them for important goals like traveling.

• Manage your credit card bills by paying on time to avoid additional charges. Keep zero balance as much as possible. Stick to one major credit card to avoid headaches when paying multiple accounts. Use debit card if it is really important.

• Pay your bills online (utilities, mortgage, rent, cellphone and internet plans). Paying them electronically ensures that you pay them on time and avoid additional charges for late payment. If you can arrange to pay them all at the same time, it will be better. Though it may mean a little scrimping on your part for a certain period of the month but it will make your budgeting free from fixed bills payments during the remaining period.

• Transfer your savings electronically from your checking to savings account. Automatic savings will make you save regularly. Select from online saving accounts like HBSD, ING Direct or Emigrant Direct.

• Use envelope system to separate your money into different expense categories. When you put funds for individual expenditures, you reduce the necessity of constant tracking of your spending. You can take your envelope intended for your groceries when you shop. You know how much remains after shopping and when you have surplus after the month, you can add them to your savings or emergency fund. It is also hassle free because you can easily track down your expenses with receipts of your purchases.

Use your fun envelope to reward yourself occasionally with something that you eliminated during the month like a cup of hot, steaming latte with your favorite chocolate cake. Treat yourself with a monthly massage because you stopped getting it every week. Buy yourself small items to compensate for expensive things you want to buy. Buy something nice and practical instead of getting the latest pair of shoes.

• To keep your budget efficient, you need to devote at least 30 minutes a week to review it. Doing weekly maintenance works is better and helps you assess the effectiveness of your efforts to spend within limits. If you are using pen and paper, list down all transactions under each category. Record the item, amount and other details you want to enter. Then check your money (savings accounts or funds for expenses when you use envelope system). Check if all your bills are paid which include your credit card and phone bills. Evaluating how much money remains in your budget will make you plan to stretch it for the remaining period of time. You learn not to overspend on things that are non-essentials.

Remember that your budget is not static. It is a work in progress. Keep on assessing its effectiveness to suit your purpose. Just don't forget that you create this budget to enjoy better life in the future.

Daniel Wells

CHAPTER 4 – HOW TO LIVE A FRUGAL LIFE

Living a frugal life does not mean scrimping on your basic needs. It is not about deprivation or sacrifices. It means smart spending, learning when to shop and when not to shop. It is about getting best deals and enjoying shopping in yard sales, thrift stores, barter boards and clearance racks. It is about having control of your spending habits. Frugal living is being determined to achieve goals and make consistent efforts to make them come true.

It is a lifestyle that is focused on conscious awareness of how you spend your money in order for you to save. It is a choice. It is a big decision to make. It requires changing your mindset to change your spending habits. Being frugal means you spend on essentials only. It means stopping money leaks that keep you from living without financial worries.

Living this kind of lifestyle gives you an option to focus on important things you want in life. It allows you to spend more time with your family. When you spend less, you increase your surplus which you can use to pay debts, invest or save for your future. You have the freedom to work less and start building a new career or business. Or you can work more so you can retire early and enjoy good life.

But remember, living a frugal life entails sacrifices. If you can make sacrifices now to have a better future, then you can start your journey to a simpler, minimalist lifestyle.

Food expenses:

• Minimize eating out to cut off expenses. Learn to cook special dishes for your family. It is cheaper to eat at home and more fun too. See how much you can save when you start doing this.

• Occasional eating out is allowed or if there is a special occasion to celebrate but learn to choose simple dishes that do not cost much. You can try newly-opened restaurants that offer discounts. Make sure that you limit your spending within your budget. And make sure also that your family knows it.

• Plan your meals before going to grocery stores for your week's supply. Maximize your budget by buying all items in your list. Buy in bulk especially those ingredients that you need in cooking. This will make you motivated to cook more and save more.

• Shop with a list. This is the most effective way to avoid impulsive buying. Stick to your list and avoid buying items just because they are on sale.

• Use clip coupons to save money for products that you usually buy in grocery stores. Shop in stores that offer coupons and big discounts to their customers.

• Bring home-made lunch at work. It will save you money and more time to relax during lunchtime. When you eat in your office pantry rather than going to nearby fast food or canteen, you save time. You have more time to finish your work early.

• Take snacks whenever you get out of home. Always carry bottled water, granola or chocolate bar, sandwich or cookies with you. It will keep you away from vending machines or convenience stores that offer carbonated drinks and high-calorie foods. Be ready whenever you feel hunger strikes.

• Reduce your intake of convenience foods which include junk foods, frozen foods and microwaveable foods. Aside from being expensive, they are also full of unhealthy calories.

• Look for freebies. There are products that offer free samples. Browse online and look for companies giving out freebies to promote their new products.

• Use freezer to store up fruits and vegetables which you can buy in bulk. Fresh foods can be stored on cookie sheets or containers to prolong storage period.

• Cook ahead. It saves time and money if you will cook enough meals to last a week. Freeze them in dinner sized portions. It will be convenient for you because you just get one pack for each meal or take them out for your lunch or snack at work.

• Try meatless dishes. Cut down your food expense by eating less meat and buying more vegetables or fishes. It also keeps you away from hypertension.

• Learn to replace sweet desserts and snacks with fresh and healthy fruits.

• Drink water instead of refreshments which are loaded with calories (coffee, juices, tea and sodas).

Transportation

• Maintain one car to reduce maintenance and gas expenses.
• Switch your SUV with smaller car if you do not use if often.
• Group your errands so you can do them all with one trip. Schedule your activities to reduce your gas expenses.
• You can also try biking or walking when your destination is just around the corner. It will keep your muscles strong and healthy which is good for your health.
• Carpool. Find friends or neighbors who work in the same district you are in and arrange carpool to save gas. It is also a great way to enhance friendship.
• Ride a bus or train. Public transportation is cheaper and more comfortable especially when you need to drive long.

Entertainment

• Cut out your cable subscription especially if your only time to watch television is during weekends.

• Borrow DVD's from your local library. Find movies that will entertain you and your family.

• Borrow books and start your reading habit.

• Cancel your magazine subscription and get information from online resources.

Shopping

• Avoid going to malls or department stores when you do not know what to shop. It may lead to impulse buying. It is better to shop when you need to buy something then go out afterwards. Window shopping will tempt you to buy more and will also make you hungry which will lead to eating out.

• Stop online buying which is easy to do. Browsing on different online stores will tempt you to use your credit cards. Just buy online when you really need to buy something.

• Use minimalist wardrobe. It means having basic jeans, pants, polo shirts, t-shirts, sandals and shoes. Learn to use plain colors which can be mismatched to your other clothing apparels.

• Buy clothing when you really need them. Look for bargains but make sure that they are made of quality material. Or you can buy high-quality clothes which will last long. Either way, your main concern is to spend less and save money.

• If you are an impulsive buyer, try using a 30-day list. The rule is to list down everything that you want to buy. Then across the item, record the date. The rule is, you cannot buy it within 30-day period from the time you write it down. Chances are you will not want to buy it after 30 days.

Living

• De-clutter your wardrobe, your garage, your house. Sell items that you do not use.. Donate them if you want to extend charity. Give them to your relatives and friends. The idea of de-cluttering is to maintain a simple, hassle-free life without physical clutter.

• Learn creative ways to give gifts to families and friends without breaking your budget. If you know how to bake or cook wonderful dishes, prepare something palatable for them. You can make homemade cookies for them. If you are an artist, you can paint their portraits or funny caricatures. Find inexpensive but meaningful gifts for them. Treasured gifts are those that connect with their passion and life. If they love to read, buy books or make poems for them. You can send them close-up or candid shots encased in beautiful frames.

• Take alcohol in moderation. When you get down to compute your expenses for your daily consumption of beer, you will be surprised on the amount you allocate for them. If you stop drinking or treat yourself with occasional drinks only, you are on the road to better health and financial independence.

• Quit smoking. Easy to say but hard to do. But with determination to attain your financial goals, you will be motivated to quit this vice. Aside from saving money, you will also save your health and life.

• Stay more time at home. Telecommute if you are allowed to do it by your company. Telecommuting reduces your expenses (gas, food and even clothing). It also allows you to spend more time with your family. It also means having more time alone and making use of your time to pursue your passion like writing, painting, blogging and more.

• Be creative and make your own or do-it-yourself projects. Instead of buying commercial cleaners, why not make your own or use practical alternatives such as baking soda and vinegar. Instead of buying new shelves, why not make them. Search for instructions on YouTube or DIY websites.

• Cut down your electricity and water bill by washing clothes weekly. If it is sunny outside, sundry your clothes instead of drying them with washing machine.

• Stay healthy. Take care of your physical, mental and emotional health. Avoid too much stress that can affect your well-being. Exercise, eat healthy food and learn to balance your life and work. It will keep doctor's bills away.

Learn to travel frugally. Buy tickets in advance or look for great deals. Consider other forms of transportation like train travel or car travel with friends. Look for cheaper accommodation or stay with friends or relatives if possible. Plan your travel ahead.

Daniel Wells

CHAPTER 5 – STEPS FOR SUCCESSFUL SAVING

The hardest thing is getting started. You need motivation to develop a realistic savings plan that will help you pursue your financial goals.

Here are some steps to help you save for the future:

Step 1: Set goals

• Short-term goals – save for emergency fund, annual vacation or buying new car

• Long-term goals – save for retirement plan, children's educational plans or down-payment for a new home

Step 2: Prioritize your goals.

Decide which are important and start allocating fund for them. Focus on one goal at a time. Decide how much money you will give for the goal every month. Make it part of your monthly expenditures.

Step 3: Find an ideal saving strategy that will work for you.

- Regular savings account
- High-yield savings account – offers high interest rate
- Money- market savings account – interest rates vary in accordance to your savings

- Certificate of deposit (CD) – gives specific interest rate for your money for a particular period of time.

- Individual Retirement Accounts (IRA) – they are insured at FDIC or Federal Deposit Insurance Corporation and provides retirement savings services.

- Mutual Funds and Security Stocks - they are investment products that can be bought through broker-dealers. They are not FDIC insured so be ready for investment risks.

Step 4: Use automatic transfers to avoid spending the intended money for regular expenses.

Step 5: Watch your savings increase every month.

When you see your egg nest growing, you will be inspired to continue saving and make your dreams come true sooner than you expected.

CHAPTER 6 – MORE WAYS TO SAVE MONEY

There are countless ways to save money. Saving becomes more fun when you start seeing your bank account growing steadily. Here are more ways to help you spend wisely and save a lot.

• Sell your extra electronic gadgets if you are not using them.

• Scout quality used home furnishings.

• Buy fruits and vegetables from neighbors' orchard. They are guaranteed fresh and cost cheaper than those available in groceries.

• Look for affordable recipes and cook them for your family.

• Always check your bills for any error that will cause you extra expense,

• Eat before shopping or going to grocery stores.

• Keep your house clean so you can avoid buying

expensive cleaners to get rid of grimes.

• Be organized to avoid buying duplicate items.

• Buy fresh fish, meat products and other produce in your local wet markets. They are cheaper.

• Plant your own vegetables and herbs.

• Make your own furniture or restore old ones with fresh paint. Repair and fix broken appliances immediately.

• Exercise at home or find free class.

• Buy used items. Enjoy great finds at very minimal cost.

• Wait for bargains and sale to buy clothes, bags and shoes.

• Swap apparels and accessories with friends.

• Tell your family or friends that you budget your money for future projects so you cannot afford some activities that they want to do with you. You may suggest alternative activities that are fun and will not cost you much like potluck dinner, barbeque party or hiking.

• Reduce your use of commercial products like shampoo and conditioners. Instead use some traditional ways to keep your hair shiny and healthy like mixture of egg and lemon.

• Buy in bulk.
• Switch from branded to generic items.
• Use phone applications that allow unlimited call and text for free.

• Listen to free music on Spotify and online music channels.

• Reheat leftovers.
• Check your shopping receipts. Get the attention of cashier when he mistakenly punches item that is not included in your groceries.

• Attend free events.
• Learn basic sewing skills so you can do some minor repairs in your clothes,

• Turn off your lights when you do not use them. Unplug all appliances when you go out.

• Recycle items that are still usable. Build something nice and practical from them.

• Organize a yard or garage sale to eliminate excess items from your home and closet.

• Learn bargaining skills to get the best deals.

• Practice paying cash. Leave your credit cards when you go out during weekends.

• Avoid temptation by unsubscribing email alerts from online stores

• Pay your bills immediately.
• When washing clothes, use cold water to save energy cost.

• Schedule your trip during off-season to get cheaper deals on flight and accommodation. Book in bed and breakfast or rental homes instead of expensive hotels.

- Regularly clean your appliances to last long.
- Buy in-season products.
- Use prepaid instead of post-paid phone plan.

Get a clear big jar for your loose change.

.

A FINAL WORD

Please Leave a Review

Finally, if you enjoyed this book, please take the time to share your thoughts and post a review. It'd be greatly appreciated!

That review and feedback will help me improve the content in my books – and make each and every one more relevant and helpful to you.

Thank you again and good luck!

Daniel Wells

www.ingramcontent.com/pod-product-compliance
Lightning Source LLC
Chambersburg PA
CBHW070418190526
45169CB00003B/1317